Skills Builders

YEAR 6

GRAMMAR AND PUNCTUATION

Sarah Turner

Acknowledgements

Every effort has been made to trace all copyright holders, but if any have been inadvertently overlooked, the Publishers will be pleased to make the necessary arrangements at the first opportunity.

Although every effort has been made to ensure that website addresses are correct at time of going to press, Rising Stars cannot be held responsible for the content of any website mentioned in this book. It is sometimes possible to find a relocated web page by typing in the address of the home page for a website in the URL window of your browser.

Hachette UK's policy is to use papers that are natural, renewable and recyclable products and made from wood grown in sustainable forests. The logging and manufacturing processes are expected to conform to the environmental regulations of the country of origin.

ISBN: 978-1-5104-2117-2

Text, design and layout © 2017 Hodder & Stoughton Ltd (for its Rising Stars imprint)

10 9 8 7 6

This edition published in 2017 by Rising Stars, part of Hodder & Stoughton Ltd
First published in 2016 by Rising Stars, part of Hodder & Stoughton Ltd
Rising Stars, An Hachette UK Company
Carmelite House, 50 Victoria Embankment
London EC4Y 0DZ

www.risingstars-uk.com

All facts are correct at time of going to press.

Author: Sarah Turner
Educational Consultant: Madeleine Barnes, Charlotte Raby (revised edition)
Publisher: Laura White
Illustrator: Emily Skinner
Logo design: Amparo Barrera, Kneath Associates Ltd
Design: Julie Martin
Typesetting: Newgen
Cover design: Amparo Barrera, Kneath Associates Ltd
Project Manager: Sarah Bishop, Out of House Publishing
Copy Editor: Hayley Fairhead
Proofreader: Jennie Clifford
Software development: Alex Morris

British Library Cataloguing-in-Publication Data
A CIP record for this book is available from the British Library.
Printed in Slovenia

Contents

GRAMMAR

PUNCTUATION

All of the answers can be found online. To get access, simply register or login at **www.risingstars-uk.com**.

Word classes

Different words do different jobs in a sentence. Words are divided into **word classes**: nouns, pronouns, verbs, adverbs, conjunctions, prepositions and determiners.

Word class	Definition	Examples
Nouns	tell you the names of people, places, feelings and things	Rohit, Adrian, Manchester, chair, love
Pronouns	replace a noun to avoid repetition	**He** played on his scooter. **That** is the best picture.
Verbs	can tell you what is happening in a sentence, as in the first example. Verbs can also express a state, and can be in present or past tenses.	She **played** a game. She **felt** tired. They **are going** to the swimming baths.
Adverbs	explain when, why or how an action happens	I stroked the dog **gently**. She won the match **yesterday**.
Adjectives	describing words, which can appear before a noun to make it more specific or after the verb 'to be'	I like to eat **spicy** food. This train is **slow**.
Conjunctions	connect words, phrases and clauses	Ruby brushed her teeth **before** she went to bed. **If** it is raining tomorrow, we will need our umbrellas.
Prepositions	show the position of nouns, pronouns or noun phrases relative to other parts of a sentence, including locations, direction and relationships in time	He put it **under** the chair. **After** supper, we went to bed.
Determiners	always placed before a noun and help to define it	**All** children love to play games. **The** teacher read **a** book.

Activity 1

Circle the prepositions in the sentences below.

a) Mum fed my cat before cleaning the windows.

b) Dad collected us from tennis.

c) Come and sit beside me.

d) Did you wait until midnight?

Activity 2

Circle the adverbs in the sentences below.

a) We will go and see the film soon.

b) She had carefully written the official letter in her neatest handwriting.

c) Don't forget to walk quietly and sit properly on the carpet.

d) Obviously there is no need to repeat myself.

e) Why didn't you open the package earlier?

Activity 3

Which pair of pronouns is the best to complete the sentences below?

a) The teacher split _____ into teams. _____ were batting; the other team was fielding.

Tick **one** pair.

they	them	☐
us	We	☐
her	she	☐
them	I	☐

b) The tins of beans were on such a high shelf that _____ had to ask someone to help _____.

Tick **one** pair.

he	him	☐
she	his	☐
they	our	☐
him	them	☐

Activity 4

Put the correct letter in each box to show what type of word it is pointing to.

N = Noun   **P = Preposition**   **D = Determiner**   **V = Verb**   **A = Adverb**

a)

The baby hugged the cuddly toy in her pram.

b)

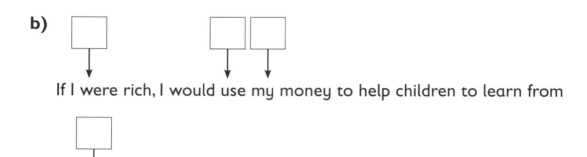

If I were rich, I would use my money to help children to learn from

education and sport.

c)

The lively puppy barked and chased its own tail enthusiastically.

d)

She gave her brother a popular computer game for his birthday.

e)

Alice sat between her best friend and her sister at the cinema.

Activity 5

Use the tables below to identify the different word classes underlined in the sentences.

a) Alyssa <u>plays</u> netball on Tuesdays, but I <u>think</u> she is much better at <u>crazy</u> golf.

Word	Verb	Adjective
plays		
think		
crazy		

b) Joshua <u>carried</u> the <u>delicate</u> chocolate <u>egg</u> <u>carefully</u> from the <u>kitchen</u>; however, Suzie <u>ran</u> past and <u>knocked</u> it out of his <u>hands</u>.

Word	Verb	Noun	Adjective	Adverb
carried				
delicate				
egg				
carefully				
kitchen				
ran				
knocked				
hands				

c) Sally <u>eats</u> <u>sandwiches</u> every day for her lunch although her <u>mum</u> wants her <u>to try</u> the <u>delicious</u> <u>pasta salad</u> she makes instead.

Word	Verb	Noun	Adjective	Adverb
eats				
sandwiches				
mum				
to try				
delicious				
pasta salad				

Investigate!

Can you use some of the words in the activities to create a crossword with clues for others to complete?

2 Types of nouns

Nouns tell you the names of people, places, feelings and things. There are different types of nouns.

Proper nouns	Names of people, places, times, occasions and events.	**Claire** and **Chris** got married in **England**.
Common nouns	The general name of things: animals, plants, objects.	He put the **plates** on the **table** near the **window**.
Collective nouns	Names given for groups of people, animals or other collections.	a **swarm** of bees a **flock** of sheep a **choir** of singers
Abstract nouns	Names of things you cannot see, such as feelings and ideas.	**hate** **happiness** **truth**

Activity 1

Underline the common nouns in blue and the proper nouns in red in the following sentences.

a) The house is on Main Street.

b) Katya played with her sister.

c) Dee went to the Manchester Pet Shop.

d) There were no yellow highlighters in the box.

e) Let's go and have a cheeseburger at Burger Bar.

Activity 2

Add a noun to each of the following sentences or phrases.

Common nouns

a) Rachel and Harriet threw the _____ back and forth across the playground.

b) Aaron was tired; he couldn't wait to get home and collapse on his _____.

c) Jemma packed all of her _____ into a big _____ so that she would be ready for her holiday the following morning.

Proper nouns

d) I can't wait to start my new school today; it's called _____.

e) Kelly shouted across the field to her friend _____, but he didn't hear.

f) David and his family were on the plane, about to set off for_____.

Collective nouns

g) A _____ of sheep.

h) A _____ of geese.

i) A _____ of whales.

j) A _____ of deer.

k) A _____ of foxes.

l) A _____ of locusts.

Abstract nouns

jealousy   trust   honest   anger   love   relaxation

m) Mel lets Sanjay put a blindfold on her and lead her to her surprise birthday present because they have a friendship that is full of _____.

n) Fatimah runs a bubble bath and puts candles all around the edge; she needs some _____ time.

o) A mother gives birth to a beautiful baby boy and cradles him; her heart is filled with _____.

Investigate!

How many collective nouns can you find? Use the school library and the Internet to create the longest list possible.

3 Verbs

Verbs are words that describe an action, happening, process or state of being. A verb can change according to what or whom it refers. The **tense** of a verb indicates when the action happened.

An **action verb** tells what the subject of the sentence is doing.

jumped, walking, drinking, goes

- Marla **goes** to the magic show.

The verb to be (am, is, are, was, were) has many different uses: as a verb; to form the progressive tense (we are walking); to start a question (Are you going to school?); as part of the passive voice.

- Chloe and Ryan **were** the assistants at the magic show.

Activity 1

Circle all of the verbs in the sentences below.

a) Stop there! Stand near the car!

b) Our team has scored another goal!

c) Pam tidied the bedroom for our visitors.

d) My birthday is on Friday.

e) Are you coming to the swimming club on Saturday?

Activity 2

Copy these sentences into your book. <u>Underline</u> the verbs and rewrite the sentences in the past tense. One has been done for you.

Andrea is <u>writing</u> a note.   Andrea <u>wrote</u> a note.

a) Jessica is sitting next to John.

b) Krish is washing his dog.

c) James thinks about dinner.

d) The cat chases the bird.

Investigate!

How many action verbs can you name in one minute? Try to beat your friend's score.

4 Subjunctive mode (mood)

The **subjunctive mode** is used for expressing hypothetical, wishful or imaginary situations. It can be used in commands and requests. It was an everyday part of Old English but is now rarely used, except in formal writing. When we are wishing or imagining, we always use the word **were**.

If he **were** properly supervised, this would not have happened.

He wishes he **were** at the rugby.

I wish Kim **were** here as she would know the answer.

The subjunctive can also be used to express commands or requests.

The headteacher demands that everyone **wear** school uniform.

Activity 1

Draw lines to complete these subjunctive sentences. The first one has been done for you.

My teacher prefers that
It's advisable that you
Tom suggested we go fishing
Her maths teacher advised
Mum insisted that Joanna make a

if the weather is nice tomorrow.
keep the bandages on for a few days.
she apply to Oxford University.
travel plan before she goes away.
we meet twice a week.

Activity 2

Circle the correct option to complete these sentences.

a) The doctor recommended that she takes/take/taken her medicine.

b) The head teacher insisted that we look/looking/looks at the screen for the information.

c) Dad suggested that I tidies/tidied/tidy my room.

d) Can you believe she insisted that we go/going to/goes to bed at 7pm?

e) It is important that you eat/eating/eats a good breakfast.

Investigate!

Can you find some examples in your reading books where the subjunctive mode has been used?

How would you use this in your writing?

5 Sentence types and question tags

There are four different sentence types. The word order is different in each sentence type. For example, in a statement the subject comes before the verb. Different types of sentences often require different punctuation.

Statements	I saw a big, scary dog near the shops.	.
Questions	Do you know him?	?
	Have you seen the film?	
Commands	Add two eggs to the cake mixture.	! or .
	Sit quietly and read a book.	
Exclamation	Stop!	!
	Wait for me!	

A **question tag** is a phrase added to the main part of the sentence, inviting the listener to confirm or give an opinion about the comment. A question tag added to a statement turns it into a question.

You have already seen the film, haven't you?

He will come today, won't he?

Activity 1

Decide if these sentences are statements, commands or questions. Tick one box for each sentence.

a)

	Statement	Command	Question
The film started on time			
Switch off the TV			
How long does the film last			
The interval lasts for 20 minutes			
When does the cinema close			

b)

	Statement	Command	Question
Where is the aquarium			
Fish live underwater			
Do not touch the glass			
How do fish breathe			
Lunch is served in the café			

Activity 2

Add a question tag to each of these sentences.

a) They are watching TV, _____?

b) He isn't working today, _____?

c) Jermaine is reading, _____?

d) You can swim, _____?

e) She can't play the piano, _____?

Activity 3

Draw a line to match the question tags to the sentences.

Jack's on holiday,		shall we?
Let's go out tonight,		isn't he?
Listen,		will you?
Tom won't be late,		will he?
You wouldn't tell anyone,		would you?

Activity 4

Circle the questions that have question tags.

a) She is here, isn't she?

b) Where is the coat?

c) Is the dog in here?

d) That fish looks like a monster, doesn't it?

e) Don't you wish it was Monday?

Investigate!

Can you find two different examples for each of the types of sentences in your school library?

Can you think of four sentences where you could use a question tag?

6 Expanded noun phrases

An **expanded noun phrase** is a group of words in a sentence that functions like a noun. An expanded noun phrase gives more information about the noun. We can add detail to a sentence by expanding the noun phrase. We can do this by adding a **determiner**, an **adjective**, or a **prepositional phrase**.

Eva ate **the cake**.

proper noun   noun phrase

Adding an adjective: Eva ate the **gooey chocolate** cake.

Adding a prepositional phrase: Eva ate the gooey chocolate cake **on the plate**.

Activity 1

Complete the noun phrase table by adding a new word each time. The first one has been done for you.

a)

			crocodile
		green	crocodile

b)

			dog

c)

			motorbike

Activity 2

Underline the noun phrases in this text.

After preparing for an action-packed night outside, the excited, expectant faces of the children were lit by the glowing, luminous flames of the open fire. A pointed, sharp-beaked northern hawk owl gliding by produced shrill squeals that amazed the crowd.

Activity 3

Look at the following passage. Modify the nouns in bold to make them into expanded noun phrases and improve the passage.

The **director** looked around the **theatre**.

"Which **actor** has left this **script**?"

"It's mine," said a **voice**.

"Come and read the **review**," said the **director**.

Investigate!

Can you find examples in the school library of the different ways we can expand a noun to create an expanded noun phrase?

How can you use expanded noun phrases in your own writing? Look through a piece of work you have written recently and see if you could add a noun phrase.

7 Phrases and clauses

When learning about punctuation, it is helpful to understand the difference between a **phrase** and a **clause**.

Phrase	A group of words built around a head word, such as a noun or a preposition. Phrases may contain verbs but do not have a verb as the head word.	some funny animals by the seaside
Clause	A type of phrase with a verb as the head word. Clauses can be complete sentences. All sentences contain at least one main clause. This can stand on its own as a sentence, unlike a subordinate clause (see page 18).	some funny animals are running round the field

Activity 1

Tick the correct box to show if the group of words are phrases or clauses.

	Phrase	Clause
at the bottom of the hill		
the dog was very small		
in a far-off and lonely village		
Maya lived in a thatched cottage		
the day before yesterday		

Activity 2

Underline the main clause in each of the sentences below. One has been done for you.

a) When she found the key, <u>we opened the door</u>.

b) Because the car wouldn't start, Dad had to ride his bike to work.

c) My binoculars help me to see despite the fog in the night sky.

d) I love playing chess even though I am not very good at it.

e) If it continues to rain like this, we will certainly not go to the outdoor games.

f) When my sister laughs out loud, it sounds like a hyena!

Activity 3

Read the sentences below. Is the underlined section a phrase or a clause?

a) <u>The child</u> who scored the most points <u>is sure to win the competition</u>.

b) <u>Before you go next door</u>, tidy up your game please.

c) <u>My brother finished his reading book</u>, after having it for three days!

d) We have an own clothes day <u>on the last Friday of every month</u>.

e) <u>Last Saturday</u> we moved into our new house.

Activity 4

Underline the phrase in each sentence. One has been done for you.

a) The sheep were led <u>to the field</u>.

b) Under the sea live all kinds of animals.

c) There is a gigantic spider under that chair.

d) Next year, we're going on an adventure!

e) Could you pass me the salt?

f) The enormous turnip grew rapidly!

g) Quickly hide the forbidden chocolate!

Investigate!

Write a definition for a phrase and a clause to display around the classroom for others to use. Can you explain the difference between a phrase and a clause to a friend?

8 Subordinate clauses

Subordinate clauses start with a **subordinating conjunction** and cannot stand alone as a sentence. A main clause and a subordinate clause go together to make a complex sentence.

subordinating conjunction
↓

I like the summer because **I can go to the beach**.

↑   ↑

main clause   **subordinate clause**

Subordinating conjunctions include: while, because, although, where, until, if, though, when, since, so that, before, after, as, whenever.

Activity 1

Underline the main clause in each of these sentences.

a) Our rugby coach said we could enter the competition if we are good enough.

b) Even though we were tired, we went to see the musical.

c) When Miss White was eating her lunch, a bee stung her!

d) If we work hard at school, we will achieve our ambitions!

e) I really wanted an ice cream although the shop was shut.

Activity 2

Underline the subordinate clause in each of these sentences.

a) Because she was late, Lauren made up an excuse.

b) Dad realised he had bought the wrong paint because it didn't match the carpet's colour.

c) Whilst we waited for my brother, we managed to spot three rabbits.

d) Gran rushed downstairs when she heard the doorbell ring.

e) Whenever we see anything with elephants on, I always ask Mum to buy it for me.

Activity 3

Choose a conjunction to join each pair of clauses.

because   **when**   **since**

a) I like to dress smartly _____ I go to a party.

b) You have been playing that guitar _____ you got up this morning.

c) _____ the train was delayed, I was late for my exam.

Activity 4

Write a main or subordinate clause to complete each of these sentences.

a) Unless you can do it faster, _____.

b) Sian went to school_____.

c) Molly bought a birthday card_____.

d) While you go to the river, _____.

e) I like the winter because _____.

Investigate!

Can you explain the difference between a main clause and a subordinate clause?

Find three sentences in your reading book that contain a subordinate clause.

9 Active and passive voice

In an **active sentence**, the subject doing an action normally appears before the object.

subject **verb** **object**

↓ ↓ ↓

<u>The man</u> drove the car.

In a **passive sentence**, the normal object becomes the subject and the subject may become part of a prepositional phrase.

The car was driven <u>by the man</u>.

↑ ↑ ↑

subject **verb** **prepositional phrase**

Activity 1

Decide whether each sentence is in the active or passive voice.

a) Mark was eating an apple. _____

b) The picture was painted by Isaac. _____

c) Tina opened the present. _____

d) The phone was being used by Mr Thomas. _____

e) The card was made by Fergus. _____

f) James hit the tree with his stick. _____

g) The man jumped off the step. _____

h) Daniel was watching the birds. _____

Activity 2

These sentences are all written in the passive voice. Change each sentence into the active voice.

a) The car was washed by Victoria.

b) The book was dropped by Peter.

c) The twins were picked up by the child minder.

d) The patient was driven to hospital in the ambulance.

Activity 3

Tick the correct column to show whether each sentence is written in the active voice or passive voice. One has been done for you.

a)

	Active voice	Passive voice
All the lions were given their food at the same time.		✓
Each of the elephants was sprayed with water by the keepers.		
The tiger walked up and down the side of the enclosure.		

b)

	Active voice	Passive voice
All of the children were given a special treat.		
The window was broken by a stone.		
Everyone was happy with the new play equipment.		

c)

	Active voice	Passive voice
The winning song was sung by the boy band.		
The bird carefully built the nest.		
The toddler ripped the book in half.		

d)

	Active voice	Passive voice
The parents watched their children in the play.		
The question was answered by the teacher.		
The fly was squashed by the chef.		

Investigate!

Can you find some examples of the active voice and the passive voice in books that you have recently read.

Can you write or explain to a friend the difference between the active voice and passive voice?

10 Adverbials

An adverbial is a word or phrase that gives more information about or modifies a verb or clause. Adverbials can also modify adjectives or other adverbs. Adverbs, prepositional phrases and subordinate clauses can all be used as adverbials. Adverbials answer questions such as **when, where, why, how** and **how often.**

Type of adverbial	Question being answered	Examples	Adverbial in a sentence
Time	When?	after we had eaten dinner	We all played a game **after we had eaten dinner**.
Place	Where?	at the new ice-rink up the road	We went skating **at the new ice-rink up the road**.
Number	In what order?	first, second, once, last, twice, never	**First**, put the ingredients in a pan.
Frequency or degree	How did it happen?	very, extremely, until, quite, almost	We left **very** quietly. There was an **extremely** large dog.

Activity 1

Underline the adverbials in these sentences.

a) Eleanor skipped down the road.

b) Jake laughed as soon as he opened the card.

c) We had curry and walked to the shops.

d) Before we went to school, we walked the dog.

e) When we got home, the cat was still asleep.

f) The team were tired after they trained.

Activity 2

Can you add an adverbial phrase to each of these sentences?

a) He threw the ball.

b) She dressed.

c) Her father fell.

d) His sister tried again.

e) He ate his vegetables.

Activity 3

Circle the adverbial phrase in each sentence.

a) My little sister Edie read in her bedroom.

b) We must hand homework in next Monday.

c) Every time we play hockey, Cole always scores!

d) I have been training with my running coach for seven months.

e) I woke up in the middle of the night.

f) You have to climb over the fence to get to the other side of the farm.

Investigate!

Can you find examples of different types of adverbials in the classroom?

How can you use adverbials in your own writing? Look through your writing and add adverbials to make your writing more interesting.

11 Tense choice

Verbs can be written in the past, present or future tense.

- The **past tense** shows that something has already happened.
- The **present tense** shows that something is happening now.
- The **future tense** shows that something will happen after now.

Activity 1

Complete the table below by inserting the correct tense of each verb.

Past tense (to sing)	Present tense (to wash)	Future tense (to eat)
I sang	I	I
You	You	You
She	She washes	He
It	It	It
We	We	We will eat
They	They	They

Activity 2

Rewrite each sentence in the past tense.

a) He can't lift the suitcase because it is too heavy.

b) This is the best cheesecake I've ever eaten!

c) The teachers are tidying the hall to get ready for parents' evening.

d) I can't see you in the crowd.

e) I am looking in the dictionary, as I don't know how to spell that word.

Activity 3

Changing the tense from past to present can make things seem more real – as if they're happening now. Rewrite these sentences by putting them into the present tense.

a) I didn't know what was happening.

b) We found her mobile phone in the cloakroom.

c) I walked across the city all day looking for her.

d) The game finished.

e) I was having a lovely holiday.

f) She seemed to fly through the air during the gymnastic display.

Activity 4

Write out a sentence for each of the following phrases. One should be written in the past tense, one in the present and one in the future.

a) watching a film at the cinema

_____

_____

b) being ill with flu

_____

_____

c) eating an expensive meal

_____

_____

Investigate!

Can you find examples of an author writing using the different tense choices?

Can you find a paragraph where an author has written in the past tense and then change this to either the present or future tense?

12 Conjunctions

Conjunctions join words, phrases and clauses together. There are different types of conjunctions:

- Co-ordinating conjunctions – and, but, for, or, so, yet

  You can run **or** you can hop.

- Subordinating conjunctions start a subordinate clause – because, as, so that, if, although, despite, unless, when, after, while, before, where, once, until, since

  We can play in the garden **after** we eat our lunch.

Activity 1

Underline the conjunction in each of these sentences.

a) When we arrived at the hotel, we jumped into the pool immediately.

b) Do we need our wellies or trainers?

c) Stop what you are doing and come here.

d) What wonderful friends you and your sister have.

e) I started to cry because I was missing my Mum.

f) There is plenty of time left but we should pace ourselves better.

g) Yes I have lived here since I was a young child.

h) Whilst we were waiting for Mum, we saw two very cute kittens in the pet shop.

Activity 2

Circle the correct conjunction to complete each sentence.

a) Mum wanted a cup of tea _____ there was no milk.

 after   before   although   during

b) The dog chased the ball _____ hid it under his blanket.

 if   and   until   before

Activity 3

Use each conjunction once to complete each of the sentences below.

until   **after**   **or**

Please can you hurry up Freddie _____ we will be late. We cannot leave _____ you come downstairs. If you don't hurry up, we will not go to buy your treat _____ we visit the dentist!

whether   **and**   **or**   **if**

Tomorrow is my birthday _____ I am so excited. I cannot decide _____ to go to the skateboard park _____ bowling. What would you do, _____ you were me?

Investigate!

How many conjunctions can you write in two minutes?

Use conjunctions from this unit in a wordsearch for others to complete.

13 Ellipsis

Ellipsis is where a word or a phrase is missing from writing but the context means the writing can still be understood. The plural of ellipsis is ellipses.

For example:

Laura stood on the station platform and she waved as the train left the station.

becomes

Laura stood on the station platform and waved as the train left.

An ellipsis sign is a set of three dots that shows words are missing.

An ellipsis can also be used to show hesitation or an interruption in the idea being expressed to give a dramatic effect.

Shall I ... um ...?

Now then ... where was I?

Activity 1

Cross out the words that are not needed or are repeated in these sentences. You may add conjunctions to replace any of the missing words.

a) Mark really enjoyed the play; Lauren didn't really enjoy the play.

b) Smoking is bad for your health while exercise is good for your health.

c) We can jump over the river, swim over the river or fly over the river.

d) The pizza was tasty, the salad was tasty, the pasta was tasty.

e) Tina jumped in the pool; Jermaine jumped in the pool.

f) The football team won the match and won a major trophy.

Activity 2

Rewrite each sentence below using an ellipsis sign.

a) "I can't believe it Are you really stuck?" asked Sarah.

_____

b) It was quiet really quiet.

_____

c) "I just thought, well I just thought it was ok."

_____

d) Then I remembered what had happened last time he saw an eagle

_____

e) Are you sure I mean really sure?

_____

Activity 3

Tick the sentences that have an ellipsis. If there is an ellipsis, write what the missing word(s) might be.

Sentence	Ellipsis?	missing words
She ran the race … I didn't.		
Ali walked to school … I did too.		
The faster runners were Caitlin and Keira.		
We went … Shazia stayed at home.		
We don't, but Samsia does like to do maths.		

Investigate!

Look through a passage of writing and note sentences where the author has left out words to avoid repeating things and to make the text read more smoothly.

Could you explain to a friend why and when to use an ellipsis sign correctly?

14 Formal and informal structures

Formal and informal styles must be chosen to suit the purpose of the writing.

- **Informal writing** is personal and chatty. (Used in a letter to a friend, such as **I am writing to ask...**)
- **Formal writing** is impersonal and uses the third person. (Used in a letter of complaint, such as The purpose of this letter is **to enquire...**)

Note: the third person uses the singular pronouns **he** and **him**, **she** and **her**, and **it**, and then the plural pronouns **they** and **them**.

she sings, they sing

In more formal forms of writing, such as information reports or formal letters, you are likely to use different words than those you would use when talking to friends or family.

Activity 1

Can you think of a formal way of saying these words or phrases?

a) cash

b) Phone you back

c) Get your money back

d) letters

e) granny

f) kid

Activity 2

Rewrite this text using formal language.

It was sort of dark in the house, and kind of smelly too. We raised a right din racing up the stairs. The gang and me'd played there all day, 'cos Dad said it were ok.

Activity 3

Write these contractions or abbreviations in full.

a) it's   _____

b) e.g.   _____

c) she'll   _____

d) &   _____

e) approx   _____

f) RU OK?   _____

Remember!

Formal language tends not to use abbreviations and contractions but informal language does.

Activity 4

Use a thesaurus to find a more formal option for these informal words.

a) cool

b) said

c) good

d) get

e) great

f) telly

Investigate!

Can you list examples of when you would write with an informal style and a formal style?

15 Subject and verb agreement

The **subject** of a verb is normally the noun, noun phrase or pronoun that is 'doing' or 'being'. The verb's subject can determine the form of the verb (e.g. *I am, you are*). A singular subject works with a singular verb.

The box is ready.

In the example, **box** is the singular subject and **is** is the singular verb.

A plural subject works with a plural verb.

The children have arrived.

In the example, **children** is the plural subject and **have** is the plural verb.

Activity 1

Circle the verbs that need changing in these sentences.

a) We was at school when the police car arrived.

b) The children always slides on the grass.

c) Jake and Ben was pleased to get a day off school.

d) If Jamal or Cody are early, ask them to help you.

e) Greg and the girls rides every Wednesday night.

Activity 2

Circle the correct word to complete the sentences below.

a) Our dogs are/were causing so much trouble in the park yesterday.

b) The neighbour need/needs to borrow our ladder.

c) Your Dad's car is/was parked outside our house now.

d) Neither Mum nor Dad is/are ready for the party.

e) Even the head teacher were/was late for assembly!

Activity 3

Tick the sentences that show the correct agreement between the subject and the verb.

a) The footballers celebrates together after the match.

b) Everyone are sitting in the hall.

c) The dog run all the way home tonight.

d) Most of the people were clapping after my performance.

e) All of my family is good at cooking.

f) The girls have been singing for over an hour.

g) The doctor pick up his thermometer.

h) The baby are playing with the balls.

Activity 4

Complete each sentence correctly by filling in the gap with **talk** or **talks**.

a) If Joe or Yani _____, send them to the head teacher.

b) The teachers and the parents _____ about us far too often!

c) Eva and Tia always _____ too much at bedtime.

d) The commentator _____ to the manager after each game.

e) "Come and _____ to me at the end of the lesson, please," said the teacher.

f) The parents _____ a lot before the school performance.

g) Mum often _____ about her family in Poland.

Investigate!

Explain and write the rules for subject and verb agreement to display around the classroom.

Can you find examples in books you have read where there is subject and verb agreement?

16 Subject, object and verb

To understand sentences, you need to be able to identify the main parts: the **subject**, **verb** and **object**.

Subject – The subject of a verb is normally the noun, noun phrase or pronoun that is 'doing' or 'being' in a sentence. The subject is normally:

just before the verb in a statement

just after the auxiliary verb, in a question.

Unlike the verb's object, the subject can determine the form of the verb (e.g. *I am*, *you are*).

Object – An object is normally a noun, pronoun or noun phrase that usually comes straight after the verb, and shows what the verb is acting upon.

The **dog chased** the **cat**.

    ↑   ↑   ↑

  subject verb   object

Activity 1

Underline the subject and the object in each sentence in different colours.

a) The hairdresser bought a new brush.

b) Sammy dropped his toy car in the pond.

c) My book is in the bag.

d) The policewoman arrested the criminal.

e) Pritika sets the table to help Mum.

f) Claire bought three oranges.

g) Dad baked a cake for Elsie.

h) The nurse carried the baby to bed.

Activity 2

Write a sentence using the subject, object and verb that are given in each row.

subject	object	verb
bus	wall	drove
squid	diver	squirted
computer	robot	controlled
candle	fire	started
dog	lead	fetched

Activity 3

Underline the verb in **blue**, circle the subject in (**red**) and highlight the object in **yellow**.

a) Matt tidied his bedroom. He washed up the breakfast things. He had forgotten to buy a present. It was Mother's Day.

b) I have flu. I have all of the usual symptoms. I have a sore throat. The room is cold. I don't feel like eating anything.

c) Sarah was nervous. It was her first day at her new school. She knew nobody. It was a huge building. Sarah had a different teacher for every lesson and it was very confusing.

Activity 4

Choose the correct sentence each time.

a) Circle the sentence where the subject is the dog.

The man saw the dogs.

The dogs barked at the man.

b) Circle the sentence where the object is the cake.

The cake was for my birthday.

Jordan ate the cake.

c) Circle the sentence where the subject is the car.

The car was a Ferrari.

The winner was the car.

Investigate!

Read a paragraph from your reading book. Can you write down the subject, object and verb in each sentence?

Can you explain the difference between the subject, object and verb to a friend?

Is and are

Is and **are** are forms of the verb **to be**. There are some simple rules to follow that will help you decide if you need to use **is** or **are**.

Is is singular: use **is** if you are talking about only one person, but not yourself (for that you use **am**).

- **He is** about to go the park.
- **She is** about to go to the park.
- **Sasha** is about to go to the park.

Are is plural: use **are** for more than one person including you.

- **We are** going to the park.
- **You are** going to the park.

Activity 1

Choose whether to use **is** or **are** in the following sentences.

a) At the moment, the queen is/are in the kitchen.

b) She is/are a good cook.

c) The king is/are no good with tools.

d) The queen and king is/are sleeping at home.

e) They is/are looking forward to a relaxing day tomorrow.

f) The queen is/are painting and the king is/are poaching eggs.

Activity 2

Use **is** or **are** to complete the sentences below.

a) _____ you having fun on the bouncy castle?

b) He _____ coming to my party.

c) The boys _____ jumping on the bed.

d) _____ you going out for a meal tonight?

e) Why _____ they so mad at me?

f) What _____ she doing now?

Activity 3

Write **is** or **are** in the blanks below.

a) There _____ many animals in the zoo.

b) There _____ a snake in the window.

c) There _____ a zebra in the grass.

d) There _____ lions in the zoo, too.

e) There _____ some young lions with their mothers.

f) There _____ a bird next to the tree.

g) There _____ many monkeys in the trees.

h) There _____ an elephant in the zoo.

Activity 4

Can you find the mistakes in the text and write a correct version?

If you wants to go to a safari park, there is many in the UK that you could visit. However, you could also travels abroad to countries such as South Africa, Kenya or Gambia. There you mights find both familiar and rare animals. Young children, teenagers, adults and the elderly is all welcome to takes part in amazing experiences that will build lifelong memories. Here are some eye-witness accounts from previous visitors:

- "Wow, we had so much fun. We saw a herd of elephants marched right past our bus."

- "We even saw a lioness caring for her young cubs. They is so fluffy and cute!"

- "Did you know that a herd of rhinos are called a crash?"

- "When a mother gorilla are feeding her babies, she hold them in her arms just like my Mum held me when I was small!"

Investigate!

Can you write down the rules for using **is** and **are** to display around the classroom? Teach a friend from Year 5 the rules.

Look back through your writing. Have you used **is** and **are** correctly?

18 Colons

A **colon** can be used in different ways.

- To introduce a list, an example, playscript or a quotation.
- To separate two main clauses where the second clause expands on or illustrates the first.

There were many precious items in the treasure chest: gold, rubies, pearls and crystals.

The treasure chest was precious: it was full of gold and other expensive jewels.

Activity 1

Add a colon to each of these sentences.

a) I eat lots of fruit bananas, pears and apples.

b) My wardrobe is full of clothes jumpers, jeans, socks and shirts.

c) There were many beautiful items of jewellery necklaces, bracelets, rings and earrings.

d) We have plenty to do on our camping trip build tents, make fires, clean dishes and cook the food.

Activity 2

Where should the colon go in each of these sentences? Write the correct sentences.

a) He quoted the famous speech To be or not to be.

b) My friends think I'm funny I make them laugh, play tricks and tell jokes.

c) Jill had to answer the question was the answer yes or no?

d) Don't forget the number one class rule raise your hand.

Investigate!

Can you write down the different times you would use a colon in your writing?

Show how you would use a colon in fiction and non-fiction writing.

19 Semi-colons

A **semi-colon** is used to separate two clauses that are very closely related but should not be joined with a colon. It can be used instead of a conjunction to join two related sentences.

Susan was warm; the sunshine was pleasant.

There needs to be a complete sentence both before and after the semicolon, but don't use a capital letter after the semi-colon.

Activity 1

Rewrite these sentences using a semi-colon to replace the conjunction.

a) I am so hungry because I didn't have any breakfast.

b) This is my favourite book and I cannot wait to buy the sequel.

c) It was extremely embarrassing in the hall so I hid behind my friends.

d) He bought a present for Gran, as it was her 80th birthday.

e) Dad treated Mum to her favourite flowers, which she loves pink roses.

f) Luke cycled to work today because he had lost his car keys!

g) You can have the last piece of cake even though it is very sugary.

Activity 2

Where should the semi-colon be used in these sentences?

a) There was an accident at the front of the school the teachers all went out to help.

b) I have found a brilliant book I can't stop reading it.

c) The explorer discovered a new plant it was named after her.

d) They climbed to the top of the mountain the view was amazing.

Investigate!

Can you explain how to use a semi-colon? Write the rules and give an example in a sentence?

Have a look through your reading book and find examples of where an author has used a semi-colon.

20 Inverted commas

Inverted commas (" and ") are also called speech marks. They are placed around the words that are spoken. Each pair of inverted commas is preceded by either a new line or punctuation such as a **full stop**, **comma**, **question mark** or **exclamation mark**.

"Would you like to come round for a cup of tea?" asked Ian.

Maddie replied, "Yes, that would be lovely."

Speech usually ends with a full stop, comma, question mark or explanation mark, which appears inside the inverted commas.

Activity 1

Insert the missing inverted commas in the sentences below.

a) Will you remember when your next appointment is? asked the optician.

b) How much? asked Dad in disbelief. Is it really £100?

c) If you have finished your work, please line up at the door, said Mr Lavin.

d) Surely you have found your shoes, said Mum, I fell over one yesterday!

e) Laura whispered, Excuse me, is there anybody there?

f) Good morning everyone, smiled Mrs Bramhall. Welcome back after your holidays.

Activity 2

Rewrite this sentence, adding inverted commas.

Why didn't I think of that! she exclaimed as she watched her brother solve the puzzle. It was easy!

_____

_____

Activity 3

a) Which of the following sentences uses inverted commas correctly?

	Tick **one**
"So when he entered your shop, said the detective, he stole some computer games."	
"So when he entered your shop," said the detective, he stole some computer games.	
"So when he entered your shop," said the detective, "he stole some computer games."	
So when he entered your shop, said the detective, "he stole some computer games."	

b) Which of the following sentences uses inverted commas correctly?

	Tick **one**
"Can you help me please?" asked the girl. "I am lost."	
"Can you help me please? asked the girl, I am lost."	
Can you help me please? "asked the girl," I am lost.	
Can you help me please? asked the girl, "I am lost."	

c) Which of the following sentences uses inverted commas correctly?

	Tick **one**
"Follow me shouted the teacher."	
"Follow me," shouted the teacher.	
"Follow me. "shouted the teacher."	
"Follow me," "shouted the teacher."	

d) Which of the following sentences uses inverted commas correctly?

	Tick **one**
Can I have a cake please? asked Billy, "I'm starving."	
"Can I have a cake please? asked Billy, I'm starving."	
"Can I have a cake please?" asked Billy. "I'm starving."	
"Can I have a cake please?" "asked Billy," "I'm starving."	

Investigate!

Write down the rules for using inverted commas to display in the classroom. Look back through your writing and check to see if you have followed the rules for adding inverted commas.

21 Bullet points

Bullet points are used to draw attention to important information in a document so that a reader can identify the key issues and facts quickly. There are two types of bulleted lists: **ordered** and **unordered**.

An **ordered** list means that a list is numbered.	An **unordered** list means that a list is not numbered.
1.	•
2.	•
3.	•

There are two ways you can punctuate bullet points correctly.

- If the bulleted items are not full sentences, they can begin with a lower-case letter. The list will usually have a colon at the end of the previous sentence.

You will need:
- some paper
- a paintbrush
- some paints.

The last item in the list will need a full stop.

- If the bulleted items are complete sentences, each one needs to begin with a capital letter and end with a full stop, question mark or exclamation mark.

Activity 1

Read the following text about penguins. Use bullet points to identify the main facts. You may need to reword some parts of the text.

Why Emperor Penguins do not feel the cold

All animals that live in very cold climates, such as polar bears, arctic foxes and seals, have large bodies and small feet, wings or, in the case of penguins, small flippers. By keeping their flippers close to the body, it is easier to keep warm. Penguins have an amazing number of feathers (approximately ten feathers per square centimetre), which are packed tightly together, acting as an insulating layer, holding in body heat and making them waterproof.

The Emperor Penguin's nose is very well adapted to the cold. The chambers in their noses reuse much of the heat that is normally lost during breathing out. Another special adaptation of the Emperor Penguin is the ability to 'recycle' its own body heat. The Emperor's arteries and veins that carry blood around the body to the extremities lie close together so that blood is cooled on the way to the bird's feet, wings and bill and warmed on the way back to the heart.

Emperor Penguins have large layers of energy-giving body fat called blubber. They are not very active during winter so they don't use up the fat. They are also very social creatures, which means they congregate in large groups, and one of their survival tactics is to huddle together to keep warm. This huddling instinct means that they do not lose much heat when they are inside the huddle because they insulate each other.

Activity 2

Write an ordered list of the equipment you would need for the following tasks.

a) making a cup of tea

b) baking a cake

c) going swimming

d) getting ready for school

e) cleaning a car

Investigate!

Find two non-fiction texts from the school library. Write down, using bullet points, the main facts you have found out about each text.

22 Hyphens

Hyphens are short dashes between two words.

father-in-law

Hyphens have many uses.

Hyphens can be used to make compound words that are used as adjectives.

well-dressed man, hang-gliding professional

They can make a verb from two nouns.

to test-drive

Hyphens are used to add a prefix to some words.

re-examine, ex-wife

Activity 1

Can you draw lines to create hyphenated words?

eye	up
part	respect
runner	opener
check	faced
self	breaking
record	in
two	time

Activity 2

Can you write a sentence for each of the words in the list below?

animal-lover   tongue-tied   monster-like   fair-haired   sweet-smelling

a) _____

b) _____

c) _____

d) _____

e) _____

GLOSSARY **YEAR 6**

You may come across some new grammar terms in Year 6. Here are some of the words you'll need to know.

Key terms are also explained in each unit of this book.

active (also see 'passive')	In an active sentence, the subject is doing the action. *Ashley found the missing key.* *The cat chased the mice.* *Lightning struck the tree.*
antonym	Antonyms are words that have the opposite meaning. *able/unable, rough/smooth, inside/outside*
bullet points	Break up large pieces of information and make it easier for the reader to pick out key details. *You will need:* • *a needle* • *thread* • *scissors* • *fabric.* *To look after a dog, you will need to:* • *provide food and water every day* • *take it for a walk twice a day* • *give it a basket to sleep in.* *How lions survive in the wild:* • *They live in groups called prides.* • *Males guard their territory and cubs.* • *Females are the main hunters.* • *They hunt mainly at night and their prey includes antelopes, crocodiles, zebras and giraffes.*
colon (also see 'semi-colon')	Punctuation used after a complete sentence to introduce a list, a playscript or an example, or to join two sentences where the second explains or clarifies the first. *We went to the supermarket to buy all of the ingredients: eggs, milk, flour, butter and cocoa powder.* *Our school has five rules to follow: one of them is to walk along the corridors.* *Over the loud speaker came the words: "Please make your way to the exits as the shop will close in 10 minutes."*
ellipsis	Ellipsis is where a word or a phrase is missing from writing but the context means the writing can still be understood. The plural of ellipsis is ellipses. An ellipsis sign is a set of three dots that shows words are missing, or indicates a pause or interruption.
hyphen	A punctuation mark used to join words or to separate syllables in single words. *award-winning, co-worker, re-enter*

object **(also see 'subject')**	In a sentence, the object is the person, place or thing which is having something done to it. *The decorator painted <u>the wall</u>.* *I ate <u>an apple</u>.* *Hannah wrote a <u>letter</u>.*
passive **(also see 'active')**	In a passive sentence, the normal object becomes the subject. *The missing key was found by Ashley.* *The mice were chased by the cat.* *The tree was struck by lightning.*
subject **(also see 'object')**	In a sentence, the subject is the person, place or thing which is doing something. *<u>A butterfly</u> flew past.* *<u>The car</u> stopped.* *<u>Hannah</u> wrote a letter.*
semi-colon **(also see 'colon')**	Punctuation used to separate items in a complicated list, or to link two closely related sentences. *I've visited Spain, Portugal, France and Italy in Europe; Brazil, Chile and Argentina in South America.* *The rain was pouring down; I put on my wellingtons.* *It was a small bedroom; I wanted more space.*
synonym	Synonyms are words which have the same, or similar, meaning. *polite/courteous, answered/replied, flat/apartment*